THE ILLUSTRATED

JOHN LENNON

THE ILLUSTRATED
JOHN LENNON

GEOFFREY GIULIANO
BRENDA GIULIANO

SUNBURST BOOKS

CONTENTS

DEDICATION

To Eddie 'The Walrus' Porter, for his many years of selfless devotion to the Beatles' elderly family members and the legion of unknown Beatle People around the world.

And, of course, to John.

INTRODUCTION

Foremost amongst the tribulations of being uncle to one so famous as John Lennon is knowing how to accurately assess the impact of someone who, at the same time is an international hero and also simply, "Our John." To be sure, John possessed an almost magical talent, but I prefer to remember him as the lanky, good natured young boy who used to tease me about my rapidly receding hairline (hair being a very major part of the Lennon family fortune as you know) and goad me for not making it down to his place in Surrey often enough. Whenever I did find the time to visit, however, it was as if time stood still. Inside the privacy of his plush Tudor mansion it was all slaps on the back, silly evenings spent playing Scrabble and lovely long dinners together tucking into some very memorable Liverpool fryups.

Although John and his dad, Fred went through some relatively rough patches together I resisted ever getting myself in the middle and hence, was able to stay friends with both. That these two loved each other devoutly was never in question. Things just got off to rather a bumpy start between them early on and left a lot of scars. It's sad, of course, but it's not really too unheard of in families today is it?

As far as the long-standing public perception of my elder brother and indeed, the entire Lennon clan are concerned, I must tell you, how ever many books, magazines or newspapers you've

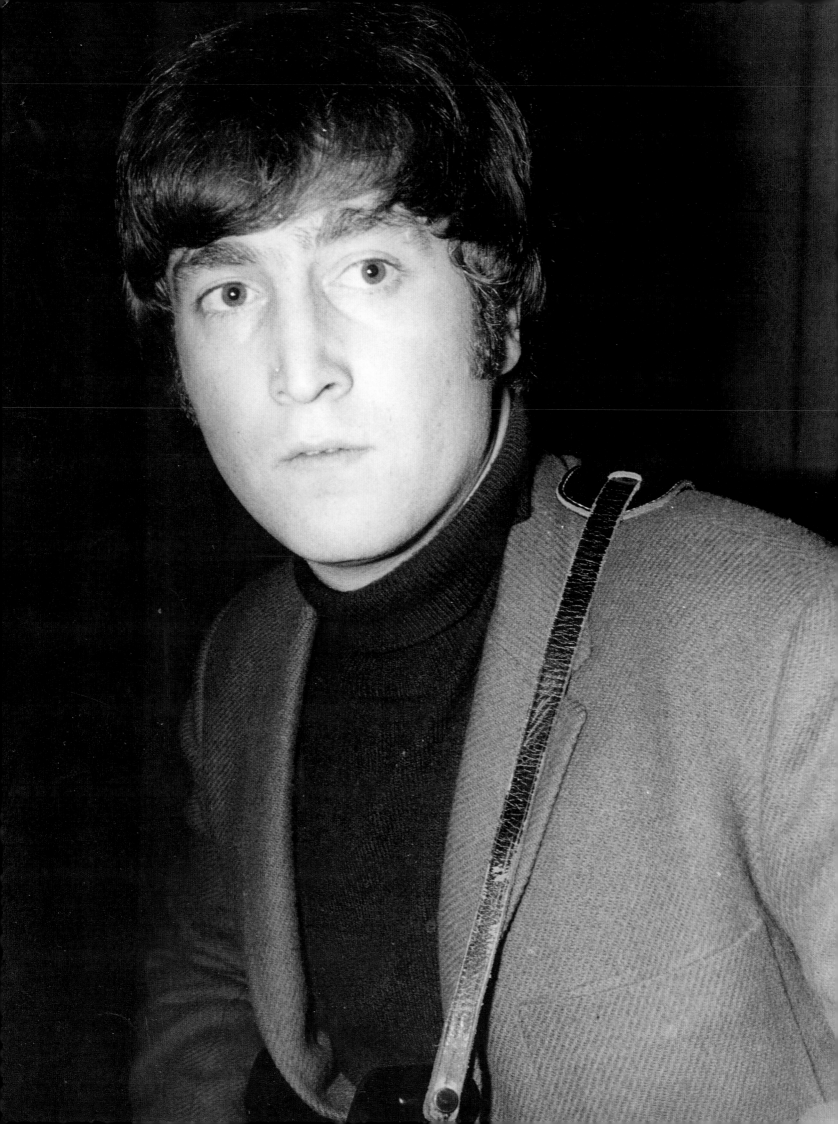

read over the years, the true story of John Lennon, the Beatles and his proud and accomplished family, has yet to see the light day. Of all the punters out there in the trenches, I must say that Geoffrey Giuliano so far out distances them all in his sterling commitment to accuracy, insight and detail as to leave all the other latter day Beatle pundits scratching around in the dust. To say that Geoffrey is the world's foremost authority on the Beatles is to subtlety understate, for my money (and I've read them all) Mr. Giuliano *is* Beatle literature.

Unlike any work ever relating to The Fab Four, The Illustrated John Lennon finally gives those who revered John a fitting record of his incredible life and times. That means quite a lot to me personally, as I'm sure it does to everyone who ever loved them.

Charles Lennon

New Years 1993, Liverpool, England

CHAPTER ONE

LITTLE BOY LOST

John and a friend back home in Liverpool

Jack Lennon, John's grandfather, had always looked forward to returning home to Liverpool to retire. Born in Dublin and raised in Liverpool, he spent many years in America as a founding member of the Kentucky Minstrels.

After working so long on the stage as a professional singer, dancer, and comedian, he finally returned home, a happy man. Soon after he had settled down in a comfortable, lower-middle-class neighbourhood on the outskirts of Liverpool's bustling city centre, his third son, Freddie, was born. Five years later, in 1917, Jack Lennon took sick and died suddenly, leaving the care of his three young sons - Charlie, Sidney, and Freddie - to Liverpool's Bluecoat Orphanage.

Freddie Lennon left the orphanage at fifteen and soon secured a respectable job as an office boy. A short time later, while sitting in Sefton Park on one of his numerous "unscheduled" afternoons off, he met Julia Stanley, a chatty, vivacious, good-natured schoolgirl whose father, George, was an officer with the Liverpool Salvage Company. Freddie and Julia went out together on and off for the next ten years, but certainly not with the blessings of the Stanleys, who considered themselves a definite cut above the careless, freewheeling, Lennon.

At sixteen Freddie signed on as a steward on a passenger ship in the White Star Line. Although the work was gruelling and tiresome, he enjoyed life at sea and quickly worked his way up to the responsible position of headwaiter in the posh dining hall of the luxurious ocean liner. On one of his infrequent shore leaves, against the wishes of Julia's family and without so much as a pound note between them, Freddie and Julia were married on December 3, 1938, at the public register office at 64 Mount Pleasant Road. The happy couple spent their honeymoon at the cinema, and the next day Freddie sailed away

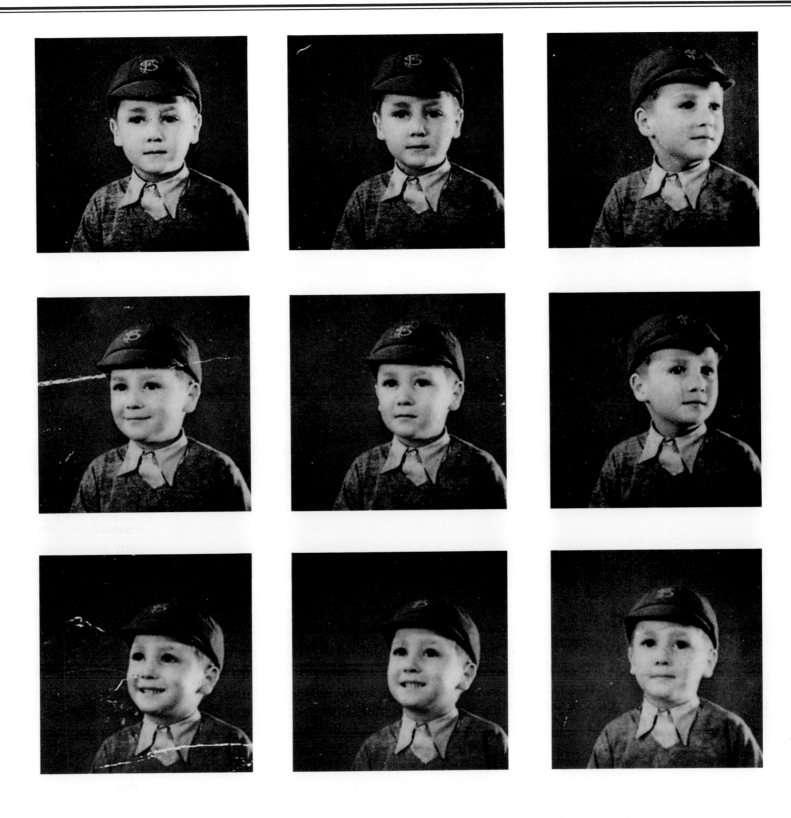

to the West Indies for a three-month tour of duty.

A little under two years later, during another of her husband's extended stints abroad, a very pregnant Julia Lennon packed her tiny suitcase and checked into the Maternity Hospital in Oxford Street. Just after seven o'clock the next morning, on October 9, 1940, with Liverpool under heavy bombing from the Nazis, John Winston Lennon was born. He was immediately placed under his mother's sturdy iron bed to protect him in case the overcrowded hospital suffered a direct hit. Julia's sister Mimi (who later raised John) remem-

Schoolboy John as a Liverpool toddler

Lennon's boyhood home

bers, "The minute I saw John I was overjoyed. I went on and on about him, almost forgetting my poor sister."

John quickly grew into a very clever, dreamy little boy. His first recollection is of walking along the Pier Head with his Grandpa Stanley. He must have been wearing new shoes, he thinks, because he remembers his feet hurt so his grandpa slit the heels with a pocketknife, making them fit better. By the time John was three years old, Freddie and Julia had called it quits, and John went to live with his Auntie Mimi and Uncle George in Woolton. "Julia had met another man by the name of John Dykins," says Mimi. "Taking John would have been very difficult for her, so I offered to look after him myself. We had no children, and John was such a lovely, bright little child I couldn't bear to see him hurt. Both Fred and Julia wanted me to adopt him, but I could never get them both down to the office to sign the papers."

John's first school was Dovedale Primary. He was a cheerful boy, full of fun and mischief, who impressed both schoolmates and teachers with his natural leadership and naughty sense of adventure. He was also quite creative. By the age of seven he was even writing his own books. One of them, "Sport, Speed. Edited and Illustrated by J.W. Lennon," contained a witty collection of poems, caricatures, and short stories that hinted at his talent as a writer with a keen sense of the absurd.

When he was twelve, John left Dovedale for Quarry Bank Grammar School just a mile or so away from his aunt's house on Menlove Avenue. Then in June 1953 his beloved uncle George died unexpectedly from a massive haemorrhage caused by an undiscovered liver ailment. His death was a terrible blow to John. His aunt Mimi believes it was George's sudden death that strengthened John's early resolve to isolate himself emotionally from things too personal or painful for his sensitive, artistic psyche to handle.

John's years at Quarry Bank were characterised by the consistent academic failure and random creative achievement of a young man struggling with the seed of genius sown in the soil of middle-class conformity. He recalls his early frustration: "People like me are aware of their so-called genius even as a kid. Didn't they see that I was cleverer than anyone else in the school? And that the teachers were stupid, too? I used to say to me auntie, "You throw my bloody poetry out and you'll regret it when I'm famous," and she threw the stuff out! I never forgave her for not treating me like a genius when I was a child. Why didn't they train me? Why did they keep forcing me to be a cowboy like the rest of them? I was different, I was always different. Whey didn't anybody notice me?"

Shortly after the death of John's uncle George in 1953 his mother, Julia, re-entered his life. Although John heard very little about her whereabouts over the years, he had often wondered about her and secretly wished he could see her again. Then when he found out that she lived just a few short miles away in Allerton with her common-law husband, John Dykins (whom John preferred to call "Twitchy"), and

BEATLES COLOR CARDS

1

MEET JOHN LENNON
Vital Statistics:
Birthday—Oct. 9, 1940
Birthplace—Liverpool
Hair—Brown
Eyes—Brown
Height—5'11"
Weight—159
Favorite Color—Green
Favorite Food—Corn Flakes
Hobby—Writing
Favorite Singer—Shirelles
Likes—Cats
Favorite Type of Girl—His Wife
Brothers & Sisters—2 Step-Sisters

©T.C.G.

PRINTED IN U.S.A.

Bubbly Beatle John back in the bygone days of Beatlemania

their daughters, Julia and Jacqui, he was thrilled. John remembers: "I started cycling up to see her occasionally, and soon she became rather like a young auntie to me. As I grew older, I began to have some nasty rows with Mimi. So I used to run away and stay with Julia for the weekend or maybe a few weeks at a time." Julia encouraged John in whatever he wanted to do. But most of all it was Julia's knowledge of popular American music that turned on John and his pals. "I started off with a banjo at fifteen which my mother taught me how to play," says John. "My first guitar cost ten pounds. It was one of those advertised in the paper you sent away for. Julia got it for me. I remember it had a label on the inside which said, 'Guaranteed Not to Split.' My mother used to say she could play any stringed instrument there was, and she really did teach me quite a lot. The first tune I ever learned to play was *That'll Be The Day* by Buddy Holly.

In early 1956 John and his friends Eric Griffiths, Len Garry, Colin Hanton, Pete Shotton, and Rod Murray got together and formed a skiffle group they called the Quarry Men. Named in honour of Quarry Bank Grammar School, the group played its first gig at the annual Empire Day celebrations on Rosebury Street. The boys played from the back of an open lorry and were paid nothing. But the day went well, and soon the Quarry Men were appearing regularly at local parties and weddings, but most of all just for fun.

Meanwhile, having long since swapped the old trumpet his dad had given him for a guitar, Paul McCartney was making progress. Always the perfectionist, he practiced everywhere – in the lavatory, in the bathtub, on the bus – even at school. A fellow classmate, Ian James, also took up the guitar, and soon the two were cycling around

Yet another boring interview

Opposite: Standing to attention on the set of *How I won the War*

Liverpool with their instruments strapped to their backs, looking for places to play. Much to Jim McCartney's dismay Paul had taken to wearing the sort of clothes a guitar-picking teddy boy might choose. With his long, slicked-back hair piled high over his forhead, narrow drainpipe trousers, and white, sparkly sports coat, he might even have managed to fool a few people! That is, if it wasn't for that perpetually innocent, choirboy face of his. At fourteen Paul McCartney was far from being a tough Liverpool teddy boy, but he was also a long way from being the proper schoolboy Jim McCartney would have preferred.

Ivan Vaughan, an old schoolmate of John's, had recently met and befriended Paul McCartney. On June 15, 1956, the two boys went together to see the Quarry Men perform at an outdoor party at the Woolton Parish Church. Paul was impressed with what he heard and remembers John singing the Del Vikings' *Come Go With Me*. "John didn't really know all the words, though, so he made up his own," says Paul. "It was something like 'Come on go with me, down to the penitentiary ....' I thought 'Wow, he's great. That's a good band there!'" After the performance Paul met the group in the church hall. He recalls his first encounter with John Lennon: "I played him *Twenty Flight Rock* and a few other tunes I'd learned. Then he played me all of his stuff, and I remember he seemed a little bit drunk. Quite a nice

On holiday with first wife Cynthia, 1965

chap, but he did smell rather beery."

About a week later Paul took a spin over to Menlove Avenue to visit Ivan. On the way home he happened to meet Pete Shotton, who informed him that John had been impressed with his guitar work and wouldn't mind if he wanted to join the group. "Sure, okay," said Paul. "Cheerio then, Pete." His first public performance with the Quarry Men was at a dance held at the Conservative Club in Broadway. After the dance was over, Paul played John a couple of numbers he'd written himself. One of them was called *I Lost My Little Girl*. Not to be out-done, John soon started thinking up his own tunes and bouncing them off Paul. And so began, very casually and with no apparent fuss, the greatest two-man songwriting partnership of this century.

George Harrison's initial interest in the guitar came about slowly. Mrs. Harrison remembers that one day she started finding sheets of paper covered with drawings of guitars among his school things. Soon afterward she bought George an old secondhand box guitar from one of his classmates for three pounds. "George tried very hard to teach himself to play," recalls his mother, "but progress was very slow and painful. I told him to just dig in and keep at it if he really wanted to learn. And by God, he did. Sometimes he'd sit up all night and practice until his fingers bled."

George's dedication to his music gradually paid off. As his fingers became increasingly nimble, he began putting together the simple, flowing rhythms that were to become his unique musical signature. In 1956 George formed his own group, the Rebels. With his brother Peter and Arthur Kelly on guitars and two other friends on the tea chest and mouth organ, they played a dance at the Speke British Legion Club for the whopping sum of ten bob each.

Talk of George's newfound musical accomplishment soon reached the ears of Paul McCartney, who would often go round to George's, lugging along his guitar for an impromptu jam session. Then in early 1958 Paul introduced George to the Quarry Men and, more important to music history, to John. "I listened to George play and asked him if he knew the song *Raunchy*," says John. "Well he did, and so I had to make the decision whether or not to let him in the group. Finally I said, 'Okay, you're in, mate.' And then it was really just the three of us from that day on."

By the time George became a bona fide member of the Quarry Men, things had begun to look up for the band, but personally John Lennon was undergoing difficult times. On July 15, 1958, his free-spirited mother was knocked down by a car and killed while crossing Menlove Avenue. "She got killed by an off-duty copper who had been drinking,"

**Ripping it up with George on tour,
1964**

John recalls. "I was just sixteen at the time, so that was another big
trauma for me. I lost her twice, and it made me very bitter. I cried a lot
about not having her anymore, and it was torture. Still, being so much
on my own at that age gave me a certain awareness of myself and a
sense of independence I might not have otherwise developed."

Around this time John left his aunt's pleasant, decidedly middle-class
home and moved into a very shabby one-room flat at 3 Gambier
Terrace with his good friend Stuart Sutcliffe. John remembers his life
there: "We lived rough all right. It was a dirty old flat. I think we spent
about four months there, practicing and painting. It was just like a rubbish dump. The others tried to tidy it up a bit, but I didn't bother. I left
all my gear there when we went to Hamburg."

John was now attending classes at the Liverpool College of Art and
soon began playing occasional lunchtime sessions with his group,
renamed the Silver Beatles, in the student lounge. After tiring of being
known as the Quarrymen, the group had been briefly called Johnny
and the Moondogs. John and Paul even performed a few gigs under
the unlikely name of the Nurk Twins. Although John's friend Stuart
was a talented artist, he had little appreciable musical ability, but that
didn't stop John from inviting him to join the group. Besides; Stuart
had just earned sixty pounds from the sale of one of his paintings and
could afford to buy his own first-class bass guitar.

By this time the group had gone through a succession of different
drummers and had finally settled on a quiet, strangely good-looking
fellow from West Derby by the name of Pete Best. Pete was born in
1941, the oldest child of Mona and Johnny Best. His father, an ex-
Liverpool boxing promoter, met his wife in her native India during the

Opposite: **At the end of a long day
during the height of Beatlemania**

Above: **Visiting a long lost relative in New Zealand**

Above: John in late 1966

Right: As Muskateer Gripweed in the wonderful anti-war spoof, *How I won the War.*

Main picture: Beatling in America in the early days

Above: **At the gala premiere of** *How I won the War*

Below: **Busking with the Fab Four, late 1965**

love with a beautiful German photographer named Astrid Kirchherr. She and two friends, illustrator Klaus Voorman and fellow photographer Jurgen Vollmer, were among the first from the artistic community to appreciate the potential that the Beatles' vibrant music and charismatic personalities might hold for a mass audience. Soon both Astrid and Jurgen were photographing the Beatles as a group and individually in various locations around the Reeperbahn.

Meanwhile John, Paul, George, and Pete were busy soaking up what they could of Hamburg's notorious nightlife. As well as sampling the strong German beer, they also became enamoured of an over-the-counter amphetamine called Prellys, which delivered an occasional burst of artifical energy to the overworked musicians and also gave them their first taste of the joys of illicit self-medication. On the Reeperbahn drugs were an easily obtained, two-bob, ten-hour vacation from a crazy world of unending sensory overload. The buxom, accommodating frauleins of the Grosse Freiheit also packed some surprises for the five basically naive scousers. Once, legend has it, while John was groping one of the more heavily made-up patrons of the Top Ten, he discovered to his horror that "she" was outfitted with an extra piece of decidedly unfeminine physiology. There were probably at

least one bloody nose, one very red face, and countless belly laughs among the boys over that little indiscretion!

Tony Sheridan, a popular, transplanted English singer with a large, faithful following among the Germans, was regarded by many as the "performer in residence" at the Top Ten, one of the best clubs in Germany. Because Tony was really a solo artist, he often used whatever band happened to be playing the club as his backing group. In April 1961, during the Beatles' second trip to Hamburg, Tony used them at Polydor recording sessions produced by the well-known German orchestra leader Berty Kaempfert. Although the Beatles had recorded a few times before, once as the Quarry Men in a Liverpool basement studio and then in the fall of 1960 at Akustik studios in Hamburg, these were their first professional sessions. They recorded eight tunes, six backing Tony and two others. *My Bonnie* and *Cry For A Shadow.* Years later these recordings became pivotal in a lawsuit brought by Tony Sheridan against the Beatles and Apple Records, but for now the sessions were an important milestone for the boys. No longer were they simply another scruffy rock band posing as professional; however rough and uneven the finished product may have been the Beatles had finally made a record!

Above left: **He's crazy. No he flipped!**

Above right: **Father Lennon blesses the multitudes, 1967**

CHAPTER TWO

A FINE NATURAL IMBALANCE

Arriving at yet another prestigious party

Opposite: At the premiere of the Beatles' animated hit, *Yellow Submarine*

Once it got going, Beatlemania swept across the British Isles with an intensity and momentum far beyond anything Brian Epstein or the Boys could have envisioned. It was hard to believe that when he first took over the Beatles, Brian had been unable to interest any of the major record labels and that it was only by the luckiest of coincidences that he landed a deal with Parlophone. Now everywhere the Beatles went, they were pursued by hordes of screaming, crying, swooning young women. And by a ruthless British press, who faithfully reported every successive outbreak of Beatlemania with the kind of coverage usually reserved for lesser news events, such as the outbreak of world war! Still the Beatles remained dissatisfied. Locked up by themselves for days on end in one lifeless hotel room after another, they talked of only one thing - conquering America!

Midway over the Atlantic on board Pan Am flight 101 to New York, the Beatles were feeling more than a little anxious about what sort of reception they would find on landing. But all doubts were swept away when at 1.35 on the afternoon of February 7, 1964, they touched down on the icy runway of Kennedy Airport. As the plane slowly made its way toward the terminal, the shrill sound of over ten thousand teenage voices chanting and screaming for the Beatles penetrated the hull of the aircraft. Peering out of the fozen windows of the DC-10, the Beatles saw for the first time what America had in store for the. "Every kid from Broadway to the Bronx was there," remembers one seasoned veteran of the quizzical New York press corps. "They were all wearing buttons that said 'I LIKE THE BEATLES' and waving banners and placards they'd made up at home. Little girls were fainting, cops were sticking bullets in their ears to help drown out the scream-

ing, and the poor Beatles were just standing there at the door of the plane completely and utterly in shock. No one, I mean no one, had ever seen or even remotely suspected anything like this!" The boys were led to the airport press lounge, where they held the largest, wildest press conference in the history of New York City. John Lennon yelled at everyone to shut up, and the entire room applauded! Beatlemania now held the entire world in its grasp as an untold number of hustlers, con men, and copycats all clamoured to jump on board the bandwagon.

After the press conference the Beatles were ceremoniously driven into New York City and installed in a palatial suite of rooms at the Plaza Hotel. George didn't like the food, but this didn't really bother the management, because it didn't especially care for the Beatles and their fifteen thousand or so screaming fans tearing up the hotel. This was rather ungraciously made known to the entire world by offering the Beatles to any other four-star hotel that would have them.

The fact that New York's innkeepers lacked a sense of humour, however, was no indication that the rest of the nation wasn't ready for a good, hearty "Yeah, yeah, yeah." Even Elvis Presley, the Beatles' rock

Opposite left: **Making a plea for peace in snowy Denmark**

Opposite right: **Although Yoko's talent was legend in the mind of her loving husband John, most of us, missed the point**

Below: **John, Paul, George and Billy? Drummer Nichols sits in for Ringo, 1964.**

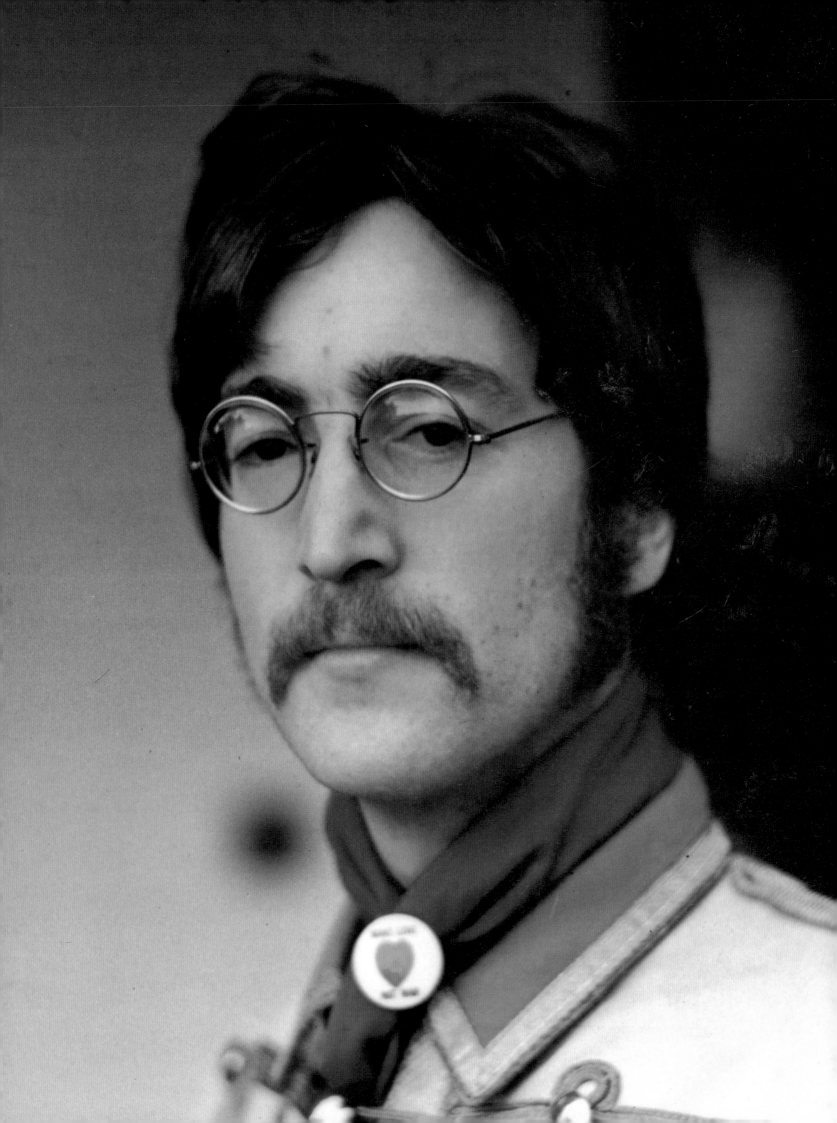

'n' roll hero, acknowledged their impact on the music scene by sending them a congratulatory telegram following their first appearance on the "Ed Sullivan Show." In fact, many newspapers were already calling for the "King" to abdicate his throne. The New York Daily News wrote, "The Presleyan gyrations and caterwauling of yesterday are but lukewarm dandelion tea in comparison to the 100-proof elixir served up by the Beatles." And so it seemed that John Lennon's longtime wish that the Beatles might one day be bigger than Elvis was finally coming true.

Despite their many triumphs, however, as the Beatles toured the United States the pattern of lunacy that constantly surrounded them began to take its toll. John and George, in particular, became very cynical about the fact that the Beatles seemed to have become an excuse for kids to run wild in the streets, smashing up phone boxes and climbing up elevator shafts in hopes of catching a brief glimpse of one of their idols. Plopped down in the middle of Anytown, U.S.A., the Fab Four were forced to perform in outdoor

The Fab Four take a break in shooting for _The Magical Mystery Tour_

Opposite: **In the studio during sessions for _Sergeant Pepper_**

Right: **He _was_ the Walrus**

sports arenas with virtually no acoustics, proper amplification, or adequate security. "The bigger we got, the more unreality we had to face," says John. "It was all just a bad joke to me. One has to completely humiliate oneself to be what the Beatles were. I didn't know, I couldn't foresee. It just happened gradually, bit by bit, until you're doing exactly what you don't want with people you simply can't stand! The people you hated when you were ten." Still the tours lumbered on, each city melting into the next, each performance more meaningless than the one before. Their ever-faithful road manager, Mal Evans, remembers they even faced being electrocuted by their own instruments when they were forced to continue performing at outdoor gigs when it began to rain. "What could we do?" he muses. "If we'd stopped the show, the kids would have stampeded and probably torn us limb from limb!" A plane carrying the Beatles was shot at by a jealous boyfriend, and Brian became the victim of an extortion attempt after a shadowy love affair with a New York construction worker. But what was worse - what made it absolutely impossible for the Beaatles to continue touring for an extended period of time - was the undeniable reality that in the midst of all this chaos, the audiences had forgotten the music. Everyone was still applauding, but no one was really listening anymore.

From February 2, 1963, to August 29, 1966, the Beatles played over 225 live shows in almost every country and continent of the free world. They performed for millions of hysterical teenyboppers, were pelted by rock-hard jelly beans, and were constantly harassed by fans looking for souvenirs - everything from personalised autographs to bits of their hair, clothes, and even fingernails. Crippled children were wheeled into the boys' dressing rooms in hopes that a dose of their mysterious power might restore or straighten lifeless limbs and twisted bodies. Airport terminals were continually soiled by young women who wet their pants on catching up with their favourite Beatle.

This was, all in all, quite a lot of madness for four provincial young men from the north of England to endure. And so, when the Beatles laid down their instruments after their last number at Candlestick Park in San Francisco in August 1966, they said good-bye to public performing forever. From now on John, Paul, George and Ringo would devote themselves exclusively to working their magic only in the privacy and sanctity of the recording studio.

The Beatles' retreat from public life into the studio gave them greater scope to express themselves musically and reduced the pressure of having to crank out one top-selling hit after another. After so many years of hustling to reach the top, the Beatles reveled in their newfound artistic freedom. One of the first and most significant manifestations of this change in direction was their concentrated effort to write better, more meaningful songs. John explains: "Beatlemusic is when we all get together, you know. Of course, we really don't write songs together that much anymore. Now it's just occasional bits, a line or two. We used to write a lot when we were touring, mainly out of sheer boredom. But today

the Beatles just go into the studio, and it happens! See, I remember our early meetings with Dylan where he'd constantly go on about the words. Well, I naturally play with the lyrics anyway, but I suppose I made a more conscious effort to be 'wordy a la Dylan' after that. When I started out, you see, rock 'n' roll itself was the basic revolution to people of my age. We needed something loud and clear to break through all the unfeeling and repression that had been coming down on us kids. Rock makes good sense, but then again, so does pure sound. Paul has always said that in the end we'll all probably be writing one-note pop songs, and he's right. But for now we're still working with the concept of 'sound pictures' - that is, creating visual images through the medium of

Above: **Exiting Apple**
Right: **At the opening for Lennons' 'You Are Here' conceptual art exhibition, 1968**

Previous page: **With young Julian at the Rolling Stones Rock and Roll Circus, 1969**
Inset: **Entertaining at the Apple Christmas party, 1968**

Opposite: **Lennon with a larger than life rendition of his birth certificate**

(PRINTED by Authority of the Registrar General)
OF

COPY of an ENTRY·of·BIRTH
PERSUANT to the BIRTHS & DEATHS ACT

B.CE

Registration District *Liverpool* in the County of *Lancashire*

if any	NO·	When & Where Born	Sex	Signature of Informant	When Registered	Signature of Registrar	Name & Surname
	Nine	ninth October 1940 Oxford St. Maternity Hospital. Liverpool	Boy	E. Right (X15)	November 1940	X. Isaac Whimp	Alfred Lenn

... Whimp, Registrar of Births & Deaths for the District of *Liverpool* , in the County of *Lancashire* . Do hereby certify that the ... of the entry No 7 in the Register of Births for the said district, and that such is now legally in my Custody.

Wes. Hand this 27th day of November 1940

X. Isaac Whimp
REGISTRAR of BIRTHS & De

sound. There's still a lot to be learned in this area as well."

Albums like *Rubber Soul* and *Revolver* certainly shook up the Beatles' musical image with their innovate use of classical orchestrations, lofty, intricate lyrics, and the virtually unheard-of addition to popular music of sound effects. And although they were all very successful, they were little more than brief, though thoroughly engrossing, sideshows to the main event, *Sgt. Pepper's Lonely Hearts Club Band.*

The album was recorded with great enthusiasm at the EMI studios between December 1966 and April 1967. The project started off with the recording of *When I'm Sixty-Four* on December 10. Written chiefly by Paul, it also featured him on lead vocals, piano, and bass. Strongly influenced by the old-time music hall sounds of English vaudeville, this song typifies the extended repertoire the Beatles had worked to develop. The second tune committed to tape, the epic *A Day In The Life,* was initiated on January 19. Using a forty-one-piece orchestra and backed by a dreamy montage of vocal harmonies by John, Paul, and George, it is the longest song on the album, clocking in at five minutes, three seconds.

John and Paul recall the inspiration for the work. "I was writing the song with the 'Daily Mail' propped up in front of me on the piano," says John. "I had it open at the 'News in Brief' section or whatever they call it. Anyway, there was a paragraph about four thousand holes in Blackburn, Lancashire, being discovered, and there was still one word missing in that particular verse when we began to record. I knew the line should go, 'Now they know how many holes it takes to ...the Albert Hall.' It was a nonsense verse really, but for some reason I just couldn't think of the bloody verb! What did the holes do to the

Below left: **Backstage at Toronto's Varsity Stadium where the newly formed Plastic Ono Band played to capacity crowds, 1969**

Below and right: **The radical left's white knights in action**

Albert Hall? It was actually Terry Doran who finally said, 'Fill the Albert Hall, John.'" Paul McCartney remembers: "There'd been a story about a lucky man who'd made the grade, and there was a photograph of him sitting in his big car, and when John saw it he just had to laugh! That's all just a little black comedy, you know. The next bit was another song altogether, but it happened to fit well with the first section. It was really only me remembering what it was like to run up the road to catch the school bus, having a smoke, and then going into class. We decided, 'Bugger this, we're going to write a real turn-on song!' This was the only one in the album written as a deliberate provocation to people. But what we really wanted was to turn you on the the truth rather than just bloddy pot!"

Another remarkable tune on the album is George's *Within You Without You*. Recorded in mid-March, the basic tracks

The Lennons stage their now famous 'Bed-In For Peace' at a posh Montreal hotel, 1969

Partying in London following a gig to promote the Lennons' *War is Over* poster campaign

In Montreux, 1969 to attend the Golden Rose Television Contest in which their film *The Rape* was entered

Main picture: Peace and Love baby!

Peace and Love, Baby!

were done by George with a little help from Neil Aspinall on the bamboura. Indian session musicians were brought in to play the exoctic dilruba, sword mandel, sitar, and tablas. George Martin helped out as overall producer-arranger as well as conducting and co-ordinating the eight violinists and three cellists brought in to add texture and mood to the track. George remembers how it all got started: "Klaus Voorman had a harmonium in his house, which I hadn't played before. I was doodling on it, playing to amuse myself, when 'Within You' started to come. The tune came initially, and then I got the first line. It came out of what we'd been discussing that evening.

The other ten songs on the album - *Lucy In The Sky With Diamonds, Sgt. Pepper's Lonely Hearts Club Band, With A Little Help From My Friends, Being For The Benefit Of Mr. Kite, She's Leaving Home, Fixing A Hole, Getting Better, Good Morning, Good Morning, Lovely Rita*, and the *Sgt. Pepper Reprise* - were all exquisitely crafted, as compelling and ingenious in their lyrical inspiration as they were revolutionary in style and innovative in production techniques.

The trendy, elaborate uniforms made for the "Pepper band" were the creation of the well-known London theatrical costumers, Bermans, with more than a little input from the Beatles themselves. At first the boys were going to dress in ordinary Salvation Army-style outfits, but when one of the tailors from the agency dropped by the studio with some fabric for them to examine, the Beatles immediately chose the brightest patterns from a pile of satin samples. Four pairs of outrageous orange and yellow patent leather shoes were ordered, and arrangements were made for John, Paul, George and Ringo to nip into Bermans to be measured and fitted for their costumes.

There they sifted through mountains of frogs, braids, medals, hats, and trinkets to find just the right accents for their pseudomilitary fantasy. Finally, the instruments the Beatles would hold on the cover were hired and collected by Mal Evans, who spent over four hours polishing them in preparation for the photo shoot. The montage of famous faces and figures forming the backdrop for the band was assembled by Peter Blake and Jann Haworth and photographed by Michael Cooper. This was a gargantuan task in itself and took months of painstaking work. Moreover, the plain, white paper sleeve that normally holds the record was replaced by a swirling red-and-wine-coloured inner wrapper designed and executed by a trio of Dutch designers called the Fool. *Sgt. Pepper's Lonely Hearts Club Band* was released on June 1, 1967, to a flood of acclaim from just about everyone who owned a record player. And it still stands today as the Beatles' crowning achievement; from then on rock, 'n' roll was no longer just teenage dance music - it was art.

The idea for Magical Mystery Tour, the Beatles' first TV movie, was conceived by Paul McCartney, and filming began on September 11, 1967. (It would have been produced sooner, but the Beatles' participation in the global satellite telecast "Our World" caused a delay.) The concept was quite simple - the Beatles would invite a select group of close friends, fan club secretaries, character actors, midgets, and cir-

John

Previous page: **John Lennon, Peace politician, 1969**

Opposite: **Lennon just after the tempestuous break-up of the Beatles**

Happy together

cus freaks to travel around the English countryside with them in a rented coach and just see what happened. Ringo, listed in the credits as "Richard Starkey MBE," was ostensibly director of photography, and although all the Beatles contributed to the final edting of the film, it was Ringo and Paul who looked after the overall production. Unfortunately, the film was not very well received by either the critics or the public after its premiere on BBC-1 on Boxing Day 1967. The London 'Daily Mail' called it "blatant rubbish," while the 'Los Angeles Times' reported, "Critics and Viewers Boo: Beatles Produce First Flop with Yule Film." Paul McCartney was definitely not amused and quite rightly commented that if the film had been shown in colour as originally intended, rather than black and white, it might have made more sense. Nevertheless, American network officials cancelled their option to broadcast the film in the United States. It is interesting to note, however, that today the film has attained cult status among collectors and is heavily traded on video cassette on the underground market.

But public acceptance of the film's soundtrack was a different matter. Released in England as a deluxe double EP (complete with a lovely, twenty-four page souvenir booklet) and in America as a straight twelve-inch LP, it immediately went straight to number one in both countries. Six tunes were written especially for the project - *Magical*

Watching Bob Dylan at the Isle of Wight Festival, 1969

Mystery Tour, The Fool On The Hill, Flying, Blue Jay Way, Your Mother Should Know, and *I Am The Walrus*. In the United States, West Germany, and a few other countries five "filler" tracks were added to round out the album - *Hello Goodbye, Strawberry Fields Forever, Penny Lane, Baby, You're A Rich Man*, and *All You Need Is Love*.

The Beatles' famous *White* album, released on November 22, 1968, was the first official group project to be released on their newly formed Apple Records. Recorded under the working title of "A Doll's House," it featured a stark, all-white cover designed by artist John Kosh with the title, "The Beatles," embossed on the front and an edition number stamped in grey ink just below. Inserted inside the double album were four 8" x 10" head shots of the Boys and a freaky, collage-style poster (that doubled as a lyric sheet) by Richard Hamilton. Most of the thirty-odd tracks were written during the Beatles' stay with the Maharishi Mahesh Yogi in early 1968, when they were still in their transcendental meditation phase. This album showed just how far the Beatles' widely diverse songwriting ability and increasing prowess in the studio had developed, as evidenced by two prominent tunes, *Glass Onion* and *Happiness Is A Warm Gun*, both written by John.

He remembers their inception: With *Glass Onion* I was just having a laugh, because there had been so much gobbledygook written about 'Sgt. Pepper'. People were saying, "Play it backwards while standing

Opposite: John was always terrific with the fans. Here he is happily signing away at a New York theatre in 1976

on your head and you'll get a secret message, etc. Why, just the other day I saw Mel Torme on TV saying that several of my songs were written to promote the use of drugs, but really, none of them were at all. So this one was just my way of saying, 'You're all full of shit!" As for *Happiness Is A Warm Gun*, I consider it one of my best. It's a beautiful song, and I really like all the things that are happening in it. It was put together from bits of about three different songs and just seemed to run the gamut of many types of music. I pulled the title straight off the cover of a gun magazine George Martin showed me. I thought, 'What a fantastic, insane thing to say.' A warm gun means you've just shot something."

By now faint cracks were beginning to show in the Beatles' inner circle. John and Paul were often at odds over problems arising in the studio, and Ringo and George were getting fed up with a lot of the nonsense that went with being a Beatle. Still, fans the world over thought

John and Yoko, rock 'n' roll's psychedelic, loving couple

Opposite: **Performing with a two-faced colleague on a TV special dedicated to British showbiz mogul Sir**

A timely message from Yoko during a 1970 appearance on Top of the Pops

Opposite: **The world's unlikeliest twins arrive in London after a late night flight**

Following pages: **Three views of John after shaving off his famous locks, 1970**

the *White* album was great and pushed it to the very top of the charts.

Yellow Submarine, the soundtrack album of their animated feature film and released on January 17, 1969, contained only four "new" songs - *Hey Bulldog, Only A Northern Song, It's All Too Much*, and Paul's rather thinly veiled plea for greater unity within the group, *All Together Now*. This recording project, while reasonably popular with fans, wasn't really much fun for the Beatles. John has said he found it embarrassing to be working on something as "lightweight" and "poppy" as *Hey Bulldog* during Yoko's first visits to the studio to watch him record. His personal standards about what tunes he would allow himself to do were very strict, and this song was only borderline material at best. Conversely, George's two contributions to the album, *Only A Northern Song* and *It's All Too Much*, were both strong, striking tunes, heavily introspective and deeply engrossing in their spacey, mantra-like melodies.

of toothpaste they preferred, the couple remained good-natured under the cross-examination and fielded many difficult enquiries with the aplomb of seasoned politicians.

Despite their well-known sociopolitical escapades John and Yoko were amazingly productive during the final hectic days of the late sixties. From mid-1968 to December 1969 they recorded four albums together: the highly experimental *Unfinished Music No. 1 - Two Virgins*, *Unfinished Music No. 2 - Life With The Lions*, the lavishly packaged multimedia souvenir of their wedding entitled *Wedding Album*, and the hard-rocking soundtrack of John's first public foray sans the Beatles, *Live Peace In Toronto*.

They also produced a number of semi-autobiographical, avant-garde films that showed their keen eye for cinematic introspection and surreal juxtaposition of time and space.

Yoko herself published a clever collection of instructional peotry entitled *Grapefruit* and recorded four solo albums for Apple over a three-year period: *The Plastic Ono Band - Yoko Ono*, *Fly*, *Approximately Infinite Universe*, and *Feeling The Space*. In addition, John produced six top-selling albums during the seventies: *The Plastic Ono Band - John Lennon*, *Imagine*, *Mind Games*, *Walls And Bridges*, *Rock 'N' Roll* and *Shaved Fish*.

By late 1971, though, the Lennons had tired of the laid-back lifestyle they were living in England and returned to New York for good. In June 1972 their fifth and perhaps most uninspired joint album was released. Aptly entitled *Sometime In New York City*, it was supposed to be a sort of *Threepenny Opera* gone rock but ended up sounding somewhat haphazard and almost trivial. Nevertheless, it represented two important milestones in the couple's whirlwind life together. First, its blatantly left-wing lyrics aroused the suspicions of the conservative Nixon government, leading to John's difficulties with the immigration department. Second, it was the last time John and Yoko seriously recorded together until *Double Fantasy* was released in 1980. Hard times temporarily subsided, however, when on October 7, 1975, the U.S. District Court of Appeals overturned a previous deportation order against John and ended his three-year battle to live and work in America. Two days later, on John's thirty-fifth birthday, Sean Ono Taro Lennon was born. "I feel as high as the Empire State Building!" declared John to a crowd of reporters. "God bless America!" For the next five years John devoted himself exclusively to looking after Sean. "It seems as if I've been under contract to produce a hit record, artsy book, or some daft film since I was about fifteen, and now I'm tired. I've made my contribution, and it's time to just cool out and be with my family," John said at the time. "I quit. Let someone else carry it on from here." Thus the self-described "male chauvinist piglet" became the world's most celebrated househusband, steadfastly shunning all offers to either perform or record.

Opposite: **As a singing duo, John and Yoko had one great asset, John**

CHAPTER FOUR

GILDED CAGE

One of the seemingly most peculiar aspects of John Lennon's extended stint as a househusband was his almost overwhelming compulsion for, of all things, baking bread. "My first loaf, I'm sorry to say, really came out quite hard" he lamented. "It's no easy trick baking a decent loaf. If it's not as hard as stone, it often turns out soggy in the middle. Of course, the great thing about homemade bread is sitting down to a slice right out of the oven. A little butter and honey and you're in heaven"!

"I must admit, I was very proud of some of my first loaves and even recorded them for posterity with my trusty Polaroid. After I finally got the hang of it, the only problem I had was keeping myself from opening the oven door every five minutes to have a little peek at how they were doing".

All such domestic affairs aside, by August of 1980 John and Yoko were back writing and recording in anticipation of releasing a new album. This was terrifically exciting news for Lennon fans as it almost certainly meant a world tour, John's first since the Beatles called it quits back in 1966. Shortly after the release of the single *Starting Over* Lennon commented on his current state of mind as regards the almighty "business" of rock and roll.

"Why were people angry at me for not working? If I was dead, they wouldn't be angry. If I had conveniently died in the mid-seventies, after my *Rock and Roll* album or *Walls and Bridges*, they would be writing all this worshipful stuff about what a great guy I was. But I didn't die, and it just infuriated people that I would do what I want. I never could have written *Starting Over* in 1975. I'm finding myself writing like I used to. These past five years have helped me liberate myself from my own intellect and my image of myself. So I could write again

Opposite: **John Lennon, a man of almost perpetual controversy**

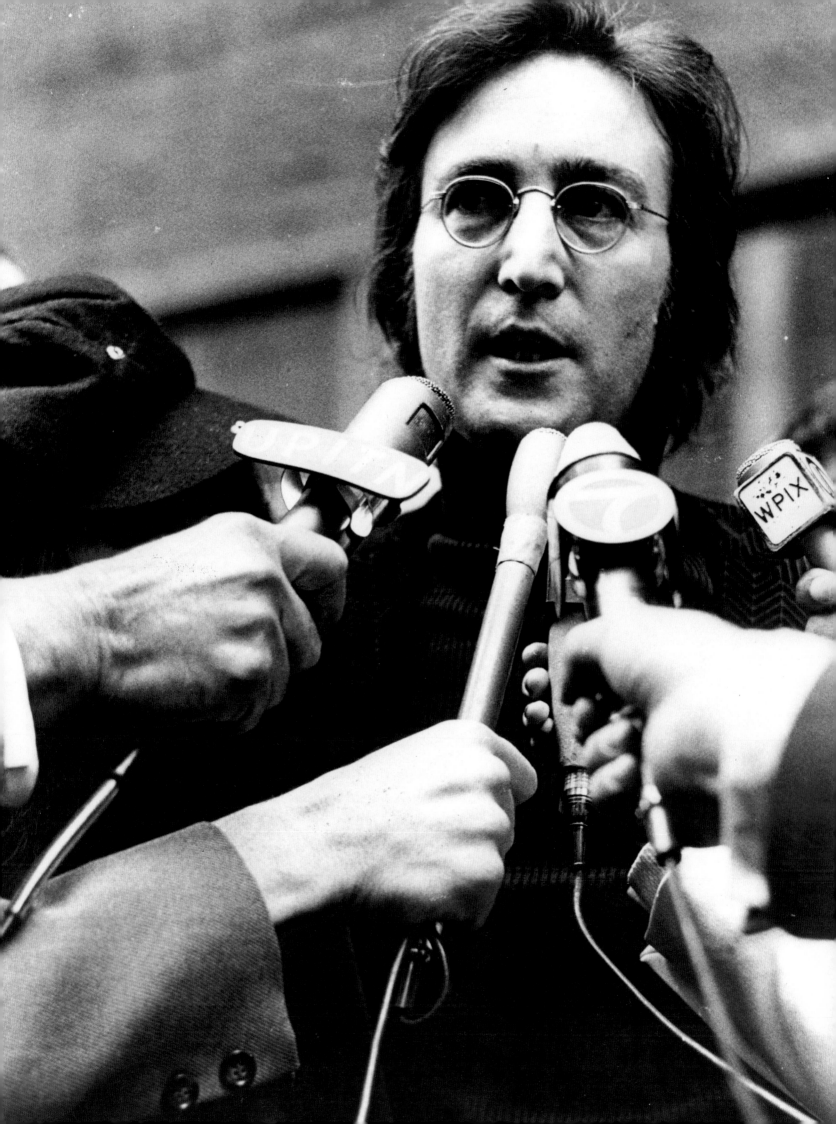

Left to right: John, Canadian songbird Anne Murray, Harry Nilsson, Alice Cooper and Monkee, Mickey Dolenz

without consciously thinking about it, which was a joy. This is like our first album. It's to say, 'Hi, hello, here we are'. The next one will verify it, and then we'll start work on the third. It's fun to be rocking and rolling now, but if it gets not to be fun, I'll just walk away, because I know I can walk away. The single is called *Starting Over* because that is exactly what I am doing. It took me forty years to finally grow up. I see things now I never knew existed".

Despite John's new found optimism, he was reportedly very nervous about the way people would react to this, his first fully-fledged artistic offering in five years. By late November 1980, *Double Fantasy* was steadily climbing the charts on both sides of the Atlantic. The ex-Beatle, it seemed, was solidly on the comeback trail.

Interwoven into Lennon's brief respite of domestic order and sputtering creativity was his often volatile relationship with the ultra manupulative and covetous Yoko. To say that John's final days inside the Dakota were needlessly bleak is to understate. So possessive and domineering was the odious Mrs. Lennon that John became little more than a bird in a gilded cage. A cage which would steadfastly hold the reclusive Beatle right up to his senseless murder on December 8, 1980. Lennon's cousin, Dr. Leila Harvey of Manchester looks back on her famous relative's passing with a mixture of deep sadness and regret.

"I wish I hadn't been so busy. I should have gone and boxed his ears a few more times. On the other hand, there is the actual business of life one has to get on with. He did send me some lovely letters, though. They were just nice and normal, not playing silly jokes on the public or anything. To me, they showed his true nature, like the good lad he used to be. Some of those letters, unfortunately, have been lost. Some, I must admit, I actually threw out because he was going on about this man who read Tarot cards for him.

Occasionally, he would send me one of his readings all drawn out in his own hand. I am sure Sotheby's would have loved them, but they went in the bin! Of course, his naughty Christmas cards couldn't ever be put up with the rest of the families.

Actually, I have had an argument with Yoko about some of those letters. My daughter felt she needed a little extra money at one point, so she nagged me until I finally gave in and let her put a few of them up for sale. I am sure John wouldn't have cared a toss, but Yoko was very rude about it. She rang me up one evening a few years after John died and really told me off about it. She implied that the publicity surrounding the letters might adversely affect a concert tour she was planning and that we were somehow trying to muscle in on her life".

Facing deportation proceedings in New York, 1972

As traumatic as John's death was for the world, it was certainly that much harder for Lennon's inner circle of friends and family. John's half sister, Julia Baird remembers hearing the terrible news. "Around about 8.00 a.m. I heard a very slight tapping on the front door and rushed to investigate. To my surprise, it was one of the neighbours come to tell me that my cousin Leila was on the phone. At that point we had only just bought the house and decided not to rush right out and have a telephone installed. "Leila"? I thought to myself, "what on earth does she want at this hour of the morning?"

Dashing across the street I ran to the phone but, strangely, stopped just short of actually picking it up. Why, I don't know. It was just a feeling of deep dread, that same feeling of total helplessness I first experienced that balmy summer's eve in 195 when Mummy knelt down and kissed me goodbye for the very last time. "Hello...." I finally stammered. "Leila, what is it?". "Then you haven't heard the news yet?" she asked. "No...... what is it? What's happening? Are your kids all right?" "Julia" she cautiously continued, "it's John. I'm afraid he's been shot." I was stunned. Although I hadn't actually seen my brother in some years, the words cut through me like a knife. "Is he all right?" I asked. "No, Julia, he's dead." "Are you coming over, then?" I said, trying in

John Lennon and his all American day glo socks

Opposite above: **With paramour May Pang at Disney World, Florida**

Opposite below: **Take two. This time with Julian**

vain to hold back the tears."

During those first few days following the tragedy, the media covered the story with a fierce devotion reserved only for the world's elite. Lennon's chiselled image was everywhere. Radio, newspapers and the telly continually broadcast details of both the world's reaction and the crime itself with deadly regularity.

Apparently, the only ones close to John that Yoko bothered to personally notify were Paul McCartney and Lennon's Aunt Mimi Smith. Yoko, herself issued a statement to the media in the harrowing aftermath of that fateful night.

"I told Sean what happened" it began. "I showed him the picture of his father on the cover of the paper and explained the situation. I took Sean to the spot where John lay after he was shot. Sean wanted to know why the person shot John if he liked John. I explained that he was probably a confused person. Sean said we should find out if he was confused or if he really had meant to kill John. I said, "That was up to the court." He asked, "What court, a tennis cort or a basketball court?" That's how Sean used to talk with his father. They were buddies. John would have been proud of Sean if he had heard this. Sean cried later. He also said, "Now daddy is part of God. I guess when you die, you become much bigger bacause you are part of everything." I don't have much more to add to Sean's statement. The silent vigil will take place on December 14th at 2 p.m. for ten minutes."

Within hours of the composer's death, both Paul McCartney and George Harrison issued press releases illuminating their views on the tragedy: "After all we went through together, I had, and still have, great love and respect for him," wrote Harrison. "I am shocked and stunned. To rob life is the ultimate robbery. This perpetual encroachment on other people's space is taken to the limit with the use of a gun. It is an outrage that people can take other people's lives when they obviously haven't got their own in order."

Adds McCartney: "John was a great man who will be sadly missed by the world, but remembered for his unique contributions to art, music and world peace."

Several other people once close to Lennon were also besieged by the

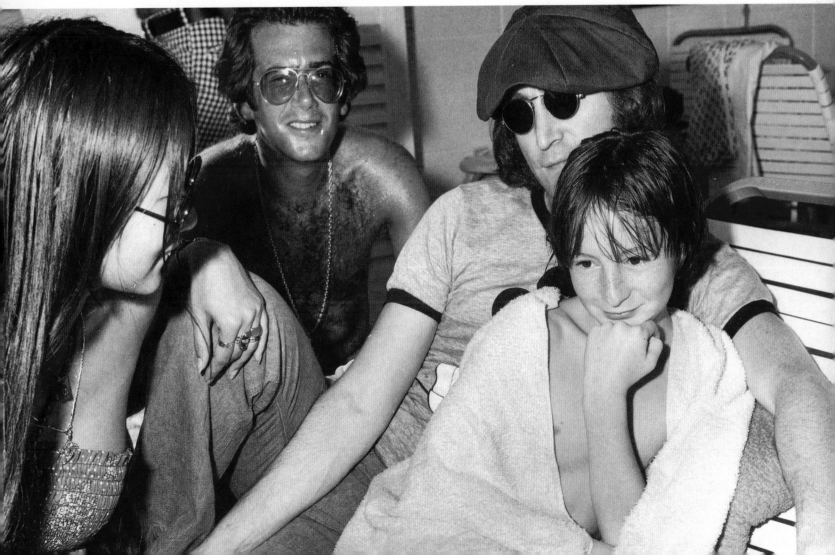